All Through

the

Years

PAMELA BROWN

Also by Pamela Brown

How it Happened: Poems

ISBN: 978-1-7367637-0-4

Preface

I have always been a writer. Even before I could write, I would write. Scribbling gibberish on endless pages, hoping that my loops and swirls would eventually form a word. (They didn't.) My elder siblings quickly learned that the best way to occupy me while they completed their homework and chores was to place me at a table with pen and paper. It worked every time.

Poetry came later, during my eleventh summer. That was the summer that I had back surgery to mitigate the effects of scoliosis. I was not afraid, but my parents were. One day my mother presented me with a floral journal to write poetry. She thought it would help me through the upcoming procedure and recovery. (It didn't.)

Writing poetry may not have helped me through my medical procedure, but it did help me through life. Within these pages are snapshots of the time I spent with paper and pen – my closest friends. Come and take a journey with me... all through the years.

Contents

I remember the day so well...

1999

Collection

dirt-covered pennies,

so easily forgotten and never to be spent.

dust covered books

on life, philosophy, and religion,

too mundane to endure.

senescent silver key

on the dresser,

warm from the afternoon sun,

shining through the slits

of the half-open Venetian blinds.

half-eaten bag of plain M&M's

spilling over onto the mauve pink carpet.

assorted colored bottles of nail polish-

some half-empty, some still full.

old tests and quizzes piled in a disorderly stack

in an indiscrete attempt to hide the grades.

but the most distinguishing feature

lies in the array of clothes,

spread in a scatterbrained manner

over the unmade bed,

waiting to be shoveled to the floor

to join the clothes that had occupied

the bed the day before.

Wallflower

Within me lives a gift that only few people can see.

I hide it from the world because it's only here for me.

When I close my eyes I can hear a voice inside,

and when all else seems to fail I just use it as my guide.

Within me lives a promise of my opportunity.

I know that if I push myself I'll build the bridge I need.

I'll set a goal, then make a plan, and follow it straight through.

Then once I've given all I've got my life can start anew.

Within me lives an inner child I haven't seen in years.

She disappeared without a trace and left me with my fears.

But if I'm strong all through this maze then after Judgment Day,

she'll come back to me once again and this time I know she'll stay.

Within me lives a hope that sometimes isn't quite alive.

It's hard to keep it living when my heart feels so deprived.

I try to keep my mind in focus when I'm feeling down-

I think of all the friends I've lost and all the friends I've found.

Within me lives a dying dream of joy and painless tears.

A piece of it crumbles with the passing of each year.

I carry it close to me as a last result device.

I'm terrified of what I'd be if I saw my dream's demise.

Within me lives a knowledge that I've only recently gained.

For so long I followed what I knew that I felt like I'd been maimed.

I kept my thoughts locked inside just like I'd been trained,

but I know now who I am and things will never be the same.

Within me lives a stream of gold with silver banks that sigh,

and purple moons with blue-green streaks hang up in the sky.

A golden gate with diamonds and jewels sits on a cozy cove,

while the endless wings of white doves flap, signifying love.

Full Moon

The moon is full and twisted tonight,

flattened by the weight of life.

How humble of him to still stand,

knowing that he is least in demand.

But I'm not nearly as humble as he,

feeble and fragile as I can be.

Still he beams down upon me,

aware of the limits my eyes can see.

Twisted and misshapen, he proudly beams,

bringing light to everything.

Flower Child

Flower child and her majesty.

Heartbreak, and it's rather sweet.

But he doesn't know what's under his feet.

Watch her-

She wants no one else to make her weak.

She will break it off callously.

Forty years and now it's on the street.

He's left standing all alone with his dreams.

His heart's broken and no one weeps.

Watch him-

He wants to be where everything is easy.

But she will break it off callously.

Tell him when he's hurt and angry.

Tell him when he has his heart on his sleeve.

Tell him all he had has fallen to his feet.

Watch them-

She wants to be on the top of the elite.

So she will break it off callously.

No Inspiration

Another piece of melodramatic prose-

God help us all.

But not a sincere thought to the page-

just a masterful twist of words

that receives a second glance.

Notwithstanding all of the skepticism,

all of the criticism that follows.

Ahh! But muses are never dependable,

are they?

Cold Summer

Cold summer.

I felt the winds blowing over my arms.

The tears were falling without my consent,

as I gave up on my feeble restraints.

My heart was blown away with the leaves.

It seems like only yesterday.

So sweet with my naiveté.

Days rolling into nights,

each taking with it a piece of my life.

The sudden realization of what others

tried to hide-

all our dreams were well constructed lies.

A dull slap to the face.

Cold summer.

I remember the day so well-

the sun shining over everything,

my heart shivering with the freeze of hell.

All of This

Save me all the particular reasons

that you think you're right.

Hate me for all the millions of reasons

that I can't fight.

You don't wanna cope with the thought

that everything that you've sought

could somehow be wrong.

And I have drawn the conclusion

that there's nothing to lose

when you are so far gone,

so far gone.

I prayed hard and there is no good reason

why I should be worrying.

It's just late now and you're not making it easy

for my heart to cope with things.

It seems I work so hard

and think I will go far,

but then I'm knocked back down instead.

And you have chosen a side

that antagonizes my pride,

and leaves me bruised and blood red,

deep blood red.

Overtaken

Never exactly sane,

all the things I wanted eluded me so.

All of my hopes in vain,

falling in time as wishes go.

And through all the years,

as I saw my worst fears,

and the sorrow endeared,

I bowed-

my courage lost in the crowd.

Free

Turn my feelings out to be revealed.

Cast my demons out so I can heal.

Even when I do

I cannot bear.

Even when I do

there's something there,

there's something there.

Don't know how I acquired most of the scars.

Don't know how I survived this far.

But never shall I weep-

the pain won't care.

And never do I sleep.

It seems unfair.

And whenever I break free

there's something else that's hovering over me.

Another ghost that's haunting my dreams,

and I'm not that strong.

I'm not that strong.

Seems by now my patience has been sealed.

Tried to transform my heart into steel.

There's something in the water

poisoning me.

Asbestos in the air

won't let me breathe,

won't let me breathe.

And whenever I break free

something from my past will hinder me,

another sin repressed in my memory,

and I'm not this strong,

I'm not this strong.

So whenever I feel free

I do not smile for fear I'll bleed.

I'll Go

How lethal all your words are,

how convincing so far-

make me almost forget the rest.

And the signals I send

tell you all I intend,

and I will accept no less.

But one more line, one more line

and I'll go, I will go.

And the ruthless things

you do to reel me in

will only let my heart down.

And a painful lesson

I have no wish to invest in,

so I'll hold my head high while you're around.

But one more line, one more line

and I'll go, I will go.

Save me the speech on reasonable doubt,

I know your background.

So every time you see me,

I'll have my guard up.

But then your willingness,

your eager tenderness,

makes me forget common sense.

And one more line - one gentle line.

Still in my heart I know you're not worthy,

and your only thoughts are to hurt me,

and move on to the next to explore.

And I've seen all the signs

that tell me your words are lies.

But more and more come,

breaking down my door.

And everything you say

makes my heart sway.

So please,

don't speak today.

Alabama Summer

Down under the great oak trees,

embroiled in a stifling heat

that only those of a

southern reminiscence

can relate to.

Chattering endlessly

with those of a generation past—

a generation of love and humor,

a generation of peace

and goodwill toward men.

Watching as the brilliant moon

conquers sky and all,

leaving us with

mosquitoes, insects, and

another midnight blue,

humid night.

Listening to the invading sound

of youthful laughter,

permeating through thick silence,

created by miles of green acres

intermittently dotted by houses.

This could be a beautiful night.

The future passed before our eyes...

2009

Eloquent Words

I spend a lot of time embedding my thoughts

into pages of eloquent words.

Divulging everything that I see,

I uncover my feelings,

and describe all my dreams.

What will I be?

What will become of my words?

When ten years have come and gone

will I be penning the same old poems?

Will my thoughts reach anyone,

or will they be forgotten?

Recurring Dreams Surrounding Me

Once again I face it-

this uncontrollable urge to interpret

what I can't even understand,

to decipher the mysterious,

the unreasonably profound.

What's not is not

and what is shall be,

so I must care not of what proceeds

around me.

But then it comes-

that paradoxical twist.

So much deeper than one can imagine, it sits

nesting its inopportune desires.

Wilt away thy deceitful heart

and wash thy faithless hand.

A stranger has kept inside of me

and led me to his land.

Monday

addled brain

progress stilted

house in disarray

eyelids gaining weight

pockets profoundly empty

television failing to delight

telephone infringing on my silence

stomach desiring that which the fridge is denying

Yesterday

Brown maple days right at my hand.

Warm summer breeze

carrying my thoughts to another land.

They were days that I knew not of misunderstanding,

and days that I cried not of painful reprimanding.

With the breeze of summer blowing

to my warm memory,

and my innocent fears awaiting

on All Hallow's Eve.

For one more day I'd give

my worry laden heart.

For one more day of youthful delight,

I'd pawn my distraught heart.

Sweet watermelon seasons sought out for months long.

Powder puff clouds a'floating

as the wind carries them to where they belong.

They were dreams that I knew not of monsters in the dark,

and dreams that I cried not of ice cream fallen in the park.

With the scent of autumn flowing

to my hollow memory,

and my innocent fantasies awaiting

on Christmas Eve.

For one more moment I'd give

my softly fading heart.

For one more moment of joy,

I'd trade my weary heart.

Down Paradise

Pale shadows getting stronger,

meeting in my mind.

This year of love grows longer;

fear of becoming entwined.

Where the road does take me

this endless wanderer shall find,

and in the end it will make me

a heartless fool both deaf and blind.

And the wind won't blow anymore,

not this far down paradise.

The leaves crackle under my shoes,

and stir up dust to gather in my eyes.

Purple sunset burdens me,

threatens to become my foe.

It blinds my weary eyes

that can barely see anymore.

I knew this road would be long,

and would strip me to the core.

When I ventured into this land

I knew what I had in store.

And the wind won't blow anymore,

not through this healthy vice.

The miles become the traveler's companion,

and the horizon offers the only advice.

Questions For Heaven

was it me all along and not them

    was I the broken one

        did I create my own hell

were you always watching

because sometimes it seemed like you turned away

    and let some bad stuff happen

am I finally strong enough

    is the testing over

why does family always hurt

Foolish

It used to be so easy-

just go and wallow in my pity.

Such was the way.

Foolish, unthinking, naïve-

I thought it was permanent,

indelibly written upon my DNA,

traced across the grooves of my brain,

immersed within my blood, within my veins.

I thought-

I believed it would never go away-

this tangible beauty of my sorrow.

Foolish was my heart.

To Losing Love

Fear that I'm besieged by an abyss so hollow.

Undoubtedly employed by former dark years.

Undoubtedly gained by the duress that follows.

Hugging a song all along that doesn't belong

to my sensitive ears.

These long-lived feelings are showing persistence,

flaming my insides with memories of their existence.

These long-lived feelings are showing persistence,

blaming my insides whenever they put up resistance

to losing love.

In That Night

We spent all our lives living in that night,

passing the troubles by recalling the love.

Then as soon as time showed us how to cry

the gold that we'd taken turned to dust.

Every moment began with the shadows we made there,

as we waited for the ache to sway,

holding everything we ever wanted

in our hearts with that day.

We spent all our lives living in that night,

pondering all the magic that we'd had.

And **the future passed before our eyes.**

And for all that we'd done nothing touched us like that.

When the rain unfolded,

when the time grew cold,

we'd reminisce on the warmth

that was once in our souls.

We spent all our lives living in that night.

The Ravine

Falling down a ravine of mystery,

the lonely voices fading in the dark luring me.

Such contradictions lulling me into a deep and lonely sleep.

Cause they love to pull us in.

This lonely hole is filling fast.

This cavern's closing in.

All lost and lonely wanderers are joining me.

Cause they love to pull us in.

They love to entice us and then leave.

Their hearts are like fire, spreading wildly

and they'll never let us leave.

Sounds of tears are floating near,

but the faces of the tortured voices can't be seen.

This haunted world is all I know as time fades.

The days fold into weeks, fold into years, fold into my life.

Cause they love to pull us in.

I'm drowning in this tomb of fear that's captured me,

and all I long for is to see a sunset again.

But they love to entice us and then leave.

Their hearts are like fire,

spreading rampantly throughout the world.

They'll capture what they see.

They've no souls, no hearts, no dreams.

It's ours they capture.

It's ours they breathe.

Far in the distance, shadows march toward me.

Holding on to my last hope, I think I may be free.

But as they draw near to me, my eyes can clearly see-

it's another prisoner, joining me.

Cause they love to pull us in.

They love to entice us and then leave.

Divinely Inspired

What if it really is me?

years and years and years

bottomless well of alone

What if it was always meant to be?

stilted growth and stunted life

passionate pleas of change

What if it was the only way?

alternate endings and fantasies

endless possibilities all fruitless reasonings

Cause what if this was all divinely inspired?

Wishes

I wish I were brave.

I wish I could say things,

and chase dreams,

and stand up for myself.

I wish I were courageous.

I wish I were loud.

I wish I could shout.

And I wish I could speak.

I just wish I could be a stronger me.

Me and Shakira

I wish I could sing like Shakira

with her raspy cat-like voice.

I'd wail about my woes,

my failed loves, my burnt toast.

I'd sing, I'd scream, I'd pound my chest

in two different languages.

I'd out-Shakira Shakira.

But where would I find her confidence?

Warm September

Warm September

This is my deepest time of year,

when all the softness of the leaves

lift away my darkened hue.

And they lift me from the ground,

floating away my tears.

It's all a poem

that's never been quite expressed before.

The words were there,

but they would not take their appropriate form.

And I feel my soul renewed,

lifting away the melancholic debris that has

formed over my heart.

Love and Wonder

Love and wonder

stuttering around my dreams,

like the gnarled and twisted roots

of a centuries old tree.

Life is changing,

rushing noisily,

as I attempt to hold on longer,

feebly gripping slippery reigns.

Minor infractions

tend to hinder me,

keeping one hand in darkness

with the light next to me.

But out of these bruises

stews a remedy,

proof of a different way.

Underneath the cruelty...

2019

In the Shadows

Under canopy

Under shade

We glow, then fade

How Will the World End

Will there be a spaceship,

metal and long,

full of alien technology,

Saturanian ideology,

blocking out the western sky?

Will that be how the world dies?

Will there be a holocaust,

nuclear and loud?

Everything goes up in an instant.

Fire burning persistent,

caught up in a mushroom cloud.

Will that be how the world burns down?

Will a natural disaster strike?

Thunder and lightning,

roaring loud and shining bright.

Gust of wind taking out the lights,

eliminating all who try to hide.

Will that be the end of all in sight?

Will hatred finally rule the day,

poisoning minds and souls,

convincing all of us we're enemies?

Will the world be swallowed up by greed?

Will the daylight turn to dark?

Will the stars fall to the ground?

Will the Lord descend from above?

Will the whole world bow down?

How will the world end?

Surrender

Where does all this come from?

Are you being honest with yourself?

Or are you blaming all your troubles on someone else?

Well if it hurts you so,

why don't you let it go?

How can we have such different views?

How can two perceptions be so askew?

You seem to be certain of your plight.

So if it hurts you so,

why don't you let it go?

And maybe this fight really isn't yours.

Maybe you should ask yourself-

has all your pain been any help?

What has your anger done for you?

Has your bitterness given you peace?

Then why don't you let it go?

Certain Truths

Some things are absolute-

no room for change,

no way to wiggle them about

until they fit the mold of our desire.

Some things can conform-

a little push, a little pull.

Voila!

A new creation.

But some things are stubborn

sticks in the mud,

and won't bother seeing matters

any other way,

resolute in their firm beliefs

that their path is the only one to take.

Like death,

some things can't be bargained with.

Because it Wasn't Really Love

It's easier than I thought-

settling,

living a life of less than.

It doesn't break my heart.

My spirit seems to be intact.

Why didn't it break me?

Giving you up-

why didn't it break me?

Wars

Separate these two hearts.

Let them drift far apart.

Plenty of wars

have been fought through these doors,

down these halls.

But dawn will always rise here,

and tourniquet each deep wound

that I might fear.

Upon Leaving the Poison

Air in my lungs.

Hope in my chest.

Heart beating, mind dreaming,

planning-

planning life, planning future,

planning happiness.

Or just peace.

Dear God, I have peace.

The End

My mind sat pondering

the emptiness inside.

My heart began wandering,

searching for some life.

Then came the end to misery.

Blue,

driving me onto a lonesome path,

filling up my heart with wrath.

Blue,

pressing me into an awful trap,

distorting life with its evil craft.

Then came the end to misery.

Then came peace.

Night became an ancient dream-no more melancholy.

Pull me from that devilry,

and bring my soul release.

Then came the end to misery.

Then came peace

bestowed unto me.

July 2019 Status Update

Half a year,

but not really.

How long has it been?

I'm at peace,

but am I me?

How hard has it been?

Where should I be?

What should I be?

Still lost, still searching

but at least there's hope

and a search for God is in place.

The Year of Me

This is the best year

that I have seen in a very long time.

Financially – though still broke

Emotionally – though still a mess

Spiritually – though still so far from home

Maybe it's the weather.

Maybe it's God.

Maybe it's the crippling depression that's gone.

But this is the year of me.

Self-Improvement

If I try harder

       I can do better.

If I do better

       I can be better.

       A better life for me.

Not that this me is terrible-

       this folly-prone, flaw-filled me.

I've grown somewhat attached.

       Grown to like, possibly love

       this error-laced me.

But even still-

       I can try harder

       I can do better

       I can be better

       for me.

The Pact

I must not allow

the domination of this heart

versus the lasting stigma

of a prudent pact.

My heart is stirred by a noble theme,

my thoughts flourishing

under a loving regime,

insistent upon my honor being restored-

my heart reclaiming its rightful place beside the throne.

A New Day

This is a start,

an opening to a new path.

I cannot bring what I left behind.

I cannot be what I was before.

Definitely Okay

I'm okay, I'm okay.

I've never been better than this-

tattered, hopeful, worried, alone,

buried under this chaotic mess.

But I've never been immune

to this doomed hopefulness.

I'm okay, I'm okay.

Gasping under this terrible weight-

destroyed, rebuilt, demolished, improved.

Under the duress of a past I didn't choose,

but accepting of this madness,

accepting of this truth.

But Maybe

Maybe it's not too late.

I'd assumed,

and I'd believed,

and I'd just settled

and made myself adapt.

But maybe…

I thought that it was all gone.

My time had passed

and it was far too late,

and I had accepted.

I really had.

But…

I believed it to be a given,

a foregone conclusion.

Everyone could read the signs.

And it was okay. It really was.

But maybe just…

I can't open my heart to hope though.

It's far too much.

Let that crashing wave of despair

wash me away

when all of it turns out for naught.

And then what's left of me?

Disappointed dreams

and tears in solitude.

All when I had made myself adjust.

I had figured it all out,

and really

I was just fine without.

But…

what if it's not too late?

Doubts and Emotions

Dove coasting over the land.

Dove floating by my eyes.

Dove blending into the blue.

Dove soaring through the skies.

Lifting away

the doubts and emotions

telling my heart lies.

Underneath the cruelty

lay a dove awaiting to fly

through the skies.

Writing is...

frustrating, debilitating,

excruciating, exasperating,

and therapeutic.

Oh so therapeutic.

When words can't be said,

and feelings can't be shown,

the paper knows.

And no one understands.

They can't see.

They just can't see

how all of it is breaking you into pieces,

and burning the remains to dust.

They can't see all of this.

They don't know all of this.

No one understands all of this-

no one but the pen and paper.

Writing is...

everything.

All Through the Years

Still in the circle,

how could I hear?

Full of the courage

when I hold You so dear.

Never the same again.

It will never be the same again.

And I must admit

there are so many fears.

Still understand me,

and my emotional tears.

Never would've made it through.

No, I never would've made it

all through the years.

You brought me all through the years.

About the Author

Pamela N. Brown lives in Port St. Lucie, Florida with her family. She is an audiobook narrator, a tutor, and a former English teacher. Pamela is a lifelong bibliophile with an obsession with the written word. She spends her free time reading, writing, and thinking about reading and writing.

Follow Pamela on social media:

Twitter - @pnicolebrown1

Tumblr – theliteratelife.tumblr.com

www.ingramcontent.com/pod-product-compliance
Lightning Source LLC
Chambersburg PA
CBHW071840020426
42331CB00007B/1796